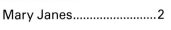

Mary Janes.........................2

High-Back Mary Jane Booties.................................3

Heirloom Booties 4

Peppermint Booties 6

Boot-Scootin' Booties.......7

Dress-Up Booties 8

Fur-Trimmed Booties 9

Nautical Stripe Booties 11

Cabled Booties................12

Fun & Funky 14

Play-Date Booties............15

Ballet Slippers.................17
Ballet Leggings 19

EASY

Sizes

3–6 (6–9, 9–12) months
Instructions are given for smallest size, with larger sizes in parentheses. When only 1 number is given, it applies to all sizes.

Finished Measurement

Sole measures 3 (3¾, 4½) inches long

Materials

- Light weight Bernat Softee Baby yarn (5 oz/455 yds per skein): 1 skein white #02000
- Size 5 (3.75mm) knitting needles or size needed to obtain gauge
- Tapestry needle
- Stitch holder
- ¼ yard (⅜-inch wide) pink and white polka-dot ribbon
- 2 (½-inch diameter) buttons

Gauge

24 sts and 42 rows = 4 inches/10cm in seed st
To save time, take time to check gauge.

Pattern Stitch

Seed Stitch

(odd number of sts)

Row 1: P1, *k1, p1; rep from * across.
Rep Row 1 for pat.

Instructions

Toe Cap

Cast on 9 sts.
Work 12 rows even in Seed st pat.
Cut yarn.

Sides

Cast on 16 (18, 20) sts.

With RS facing, pick up and knit 8 (8, 10) sts evenly spaced along right side of toe cap piece, work in seed st across 9 sts of toe top, pick up and knit 8 (8, 10) sts evenly spaced along left side of toe cap piece, cast on 16 (18, 20) sts. (57, 61, 69 sts)

Continue even in Seed st pat as established, until sides measure approx 1 inch, ending with a WS row.

Next row (RS): Bind off 24 (26, 30) sts, work in Seed st across next 9 sts (including st left from bind-off), bind off rem 24 (26, 30) sts. (9 sts)

Cut yarn.

Sole

Hold bootie with WS facing, join yarn and work even in Seed st on rem 9 sts until sole measures approx 3 (3¾, 4½) inches. Place sts on holder for heel. **Note:** *Sole should be slightly shorter than sides.*

Assembly

Sew sides of bootie, slightly stretched, to edges of sole wrapping end of sides around heel edge of sole to meet in the center. Adjust length of sole if necessary and bind off sts. Join heel seam.

Strap
Left Bootie

On right hand side of bootie, measure approx ½ (¾, ¾) inch, from cast-on edge of toe cap. Pick up and knit 3 sts for strap. Work in Seed st until strap measures approx 2½ inches from beg. Bind off.

Right Bootie

Work as for left bootie, picking up sts from left side of bootie.

Finishing

Attach buttons, sewing through strap and bootie. Cut ribbon in half and tie each half in bow. Referring to photo for placement, sew 1 bow to top of each bootie.

High-Back Mary Jane Booties

EASY

Sizes

3 (6–9, 9–12) months
Instructions are given for smallest size, with larger sizes in parentheses. When only 1 number is given, it applies to all sizes.

Finished Measurement

Sole measures 3 (3½, 4½) inches

Materials

- Fine weight TLC Wiggles yarn (3.5 oz/250 yds per skein):1 skein light pink #414
- Size 6 (4.25mm) knitting needles or size needed to obtain gauge
- Size F (3.75mm) crochet hook
- Stitch marker
- Tapestry needle
- 2 (5⁄16-inch diameter) buttons

Gauge

20 sts and 32 rows = 4 inches/10cm in St st
To save time, take time to check gauge.

Special Abbreviations

M1 (Make 1):
Insert LH needle under horizontal thread between st just worked and next st, k1-tbl.

Pattern Stitch

Seed Stitch:
(odd number of sts)
Row 1: P1, *k1, 1; rep from * across.
Rep Row 1 for pat.

Instructions

Sole

Cast on 27 (33, 39) sts.

Working in St st, k13 (16, 19) sts, place marker, k14 (17, 20) sts.

Purl 1 row.

Inc row (RS): K2, M1, knit to marker, M1, slip marker, k1, M1, knit to last 2 sts, M1, k2. (31, 37, 43 sts)

Rep Inc row [every other row] twice. (39, 45, 51 sts)

Work 5 (5, 7) rows even in St st.

Shape Top

Dec row (RS): Knit to within 6 sts of marker, [ssk] 3 times, k1, [k2tog] 3 times, knit across. (33, 39, 45 sts)

Rep Dec row [every other row] once. (27, 33, 39 sts)

Work 1 row even.

Next row (RS): K5, bind off 17 (23, 29) sts, knit rem sts. (5 sts on each side for ankle straps)

First Strap

P1, [k1, p1] twice; cast on 10 sts. (15 sts)

Work in Seed st until strap measures approx ½ inch.

Bind off, leaving long tail for button loop.

2nd Strap

With WS facing, join yarn to rem sts.

P1, [k1, p1] twice; cast on 10 sts. (15 sts)

Work in Seed st until strap measures approx ½ inch.

Bind off, leaving long tail for button loop.

Finishing

Fold bootie in half, beg at strap edge, and sew heel seam. Sew cast-on edges tog along center bottom.

With crochet hook, ch 5, using long tail to create button loop. Fasten off and sew to other edge of strap. Sew button opposite button loop.

Heirloom Booties

INTERMEDIATE

Sizes

3–6 (6–9, 9–12) months
Instructions are given for smallest size, with larger sizes in parentheses. When only 1 number is given, it applies to all sizes.

Finished Measurement

Sole measures 3 (3¾, 4½) inches

Materials

- Light weight Bernat Softee Baby yarn (5 oz/455 yds per skein): 1 skein pale blue #02002

  3 LIGHT

- Size 6 (4.25mm) knitting needles or size needed to obtain gauge
- Size 4 (3.5mm) knitting needles
- Tapestry needle
- 1 yd (⅛-inch wide) ribbon

Gauge

22 sts and 30 rows = 4 inches/10cm in St st on larger needles
To save time, take time to check gauge.

Special Stitch

Waterfall Lace Pattern

(multiple of 6 sts + 3 increasing to multiple of 7 sts + 3 on Rows 3–5)

Row 1 (WS): K3, *p3, k3; rep from * across row.

Row 2: P3, *k3, yo, p3; rep from * across row.

Row 3: K3, *p4, k3; rep from * across row.

Row 4: P3, *k1, k2tog, yo, k1, p3; rep from * across row.

Row 5: K3, *p2, p2tog, k3; rep from * across row.

Row 6: P3, *k1, yo, k2tog, p3; rep from *.

Rep Rows 1–6 for pat.

Instructions

Cuff

Ruffle

With smaller needles, loosely cast on 99 (99, 117) sts.

Row 1 (RS): *K1, k2tog; rep from * across. (66, 66, 78 sts)

Row 2: *P2tog; rep from * across. (33, 33, 39 sts)

Row 3: Knit across.

Work [Rows 1–6 of Waterfall Lace pat] 3 times.

Note: Cuff should measure approx 2½ inches.

Change to larger needles.

Next row (WS): [P7 (7, 3), p2tog] 3 (3, 7) times, p6 (6, 4) sts. (30, 30, 32 sts)

Eyelet row (RS): K2 (2, 1), *k2tog, yo; rep from * to last 2 (2, 1) sts, k2 (2, 1).

Next row: Purl across.

Shape Instep

Next row (RS): Knit across.

Next row: P21 (21, 22), turn, leaving rem sts unworked.

Next row: K12, turn, leaving rem sts unworked.

Work in St st on these 12 sts for 9 (11, 13) rows.

Next row (RS): K1, ssk, knit to last 3 sts, k2tog, k1. (10 sts)

Next row: Purl across.

Rep last two rows. (8 sts)

Cut yarn.

With WS facing, join yarn to 9 (9, 10) sts on LH needle and purl across.

Next row (RS): K9 (9, 10) sts, pick up and knit 10 (12, 13) sts evenly spaced across right side of instep, knit across 8 sts, pick up and knit 10 (12, 13) sts evenly spaced across left side of instep, knit across rem 9 (9, 10) sts. (46, 50, 54 sts)

Next row: Purl across.

Work 4 (6, 6) rows in St st.

Shape Foot

Row 1 (RS): K1, skp, k15 (17, 19), skp, k6, k2tog, k15 (17, 19), k2tog, k1. (42, 46, 50 sts)

Row 2: Knit across.

Row 3: K1, skp, k14 (16, 18), skp, k4, k2tog, k14 (16, 18), k2tog, k1. (38, 42, 46 sts)

Row 4: Knit across.

Row 5: K1, skp, k13 (15, 17), skp, k2, k2tog, k13 (15, 17), k2tog, k1. (34, 38, 42 sts)

Row 6: Knit across.

Row 7: K1, skp, k12 (14, 16), skp, k2tog, k12 (14, 16), k2tog, k1. (30, 34, 38 sts)

Bind off.

Finishing

Sew foot and back seam. Cut ribbon into two 18-inch lengths. Weave one length of ribbon through eyelet row of each bootie and tie in bow.

Peppermint Booties

INTERMEDIATE

Sizes

3–6 (6–9, 9–12) months
Instructions are given for smallest size, with larger sizes in parentheses. When only 1 number is given, it applies to all sizes.

Finished Measurement

Sole measures 3 (3½, 4½) inches

Materials

- Light weight Bernat Softee Baby yarn (5 oz/455 yds per skein): 1 skein each white #02000 (A), prettiest pink #30205 (B) and mint #02004 (C)
- Size 4 (3.5mm) knitting needles
- Size 6 (4.25mm) knitting needles or size needed to obtain gauge
- Tapestry needle

Gauge

22 sts and 30 rows = 4 inches/10cm in St st with larger needles
To save time, take time to check gauge.

Instructions

Cuff

With smaller needles and C, cast on 30 (30, 32) sts.

Change to B, and work in K1, P1 Rib for approx 1½ inches, ending with a WS row.

Change to larger needles and A.

Next row (RS): Knit across.

Next row: Purl across.

Shape Instep

Next row (RS): Knit across.

Next row: P21 (21, 22), turn, leaving rem sts unworked.

Next row: K12, turn, leaving rem sts unworked.

Work in St st on these 12 sts for 9 (11, 13) rows.

Next row (RS): K1, ssk, knit to last 3 sts, k2tog, k1. (10 sts)

Next row: Purl across.

Rep last two rows. (8 sts)

Cut yarn.

With WS facing, join A to 9 (9, 10) sts on LH needle and purl across.

Next row (RS): K9 (9, 10), pick up and knit 10 (12, 13) sts evenly spaced across right side of instep, knit across 8 sts, pick up and knit 10 (12, 13) sts evenly spaced across left side of instep, knit across rem 9 (9, 10) sts. (46, 50, 54 sts)

Next row (WS): Change to C, knit across.

Next row (RS): K3B, * k1C, k3B; rep from * to last 3 sts, k1C, k2B.

Next row: P2B, * p1C, p3B; rep from * across.

[Rep last 2 rows] 1 (2, 2) times.

Cut B.

Shape Foot

Row 1 (RS): With C, K1, skp, k15 (17, 19), skp, k6, k2tog, k15 (17, 19), k2tog, k1. (42, 46, 50 sts)

Row 2: Knit across.

Row 3: K1, skp, k14 (16, 18), skp, k4 k2tog, k14 (16, 18), k2tog, k1. (38, 42, 46 sts)

Row 4: Knit across.

Row 5: K1, skp, k13 (15, 17), skp, k2, k2tog, k13 (15, 17), k2tog, k1. (34, 38, 42 sts)

Row 6: Knit across.

Row 7: K1, skp, k12 (14, 16), skp, k2tog, k12 (14, 16), k2tog, k1. (30, 34, 38 sts)

Bind off.

Finishing

Sew foot and back seam.

With 1 strand each of B and C, make one 1-inch pompom (see page 21) for each bootie. Referring to photo, sew to front of bootie.

Boot-Scootin' Booties

BEGINNER

Sizes

Newborn (3–6, 6–9) months
Instructions are given for smallest size, with larger sizes in parentheses. When only 1 number is given, it applies to all sizes.

Finished Measurement

Sole, approx 3 (3½, 4) inches

Materials

- Light weight Bernat Softee Baby yarn (5 oz/455 yds per skein): 1 skein each pale blue #02002 (A) and lemon #02003 (B)
- Size 6 (4.25mm) knitting needles or size needed to obtain gauge
- Tapestry needle

Gauge

20 sts and 44 rows = 4 inches/10cm in garter st
To save time, take time to check gauge.

Instructions

With B, cast on 30 (36, 40) sts.

Work in Garter st until piece measures approx 1½ (2, 2) inches from beg, ending with a WS row.

Next row (RS): K1, k2tog, knit to last 3 sts, k2tog, k1. (28, 34, 38 sts)

Rep last row. (26, 32, 36 sts)

Bind off 6 (7, 7) sts at beg of next 2 rows. (14, 18, 22 sts)

Change to A, and work even for 1 (1½, 1½) inches.

Bind off.

Finishing

Fold piece in half and sew sole, toe, and top seams leaving cuff un-sewn. Fold back cuff.

Make twisted cord (see page 21) with 1 strand each of A and B. For each bootie, cut 2 (4-inch) lengths of twisted cord. Attach one length to each side of center opening and tie into a bow.

For each bootie, make 2 1-inch pompoms (see page 21) using 1 strand each of A and B. Attach pompoms to ends of each cord.

Dress-Up Booties

EASY

Sizes

Newborn (3–6, 6–9) months
Instructions are given for smallest size, with larger sizes in parentheses. When only 1 number is given, it applies to all sizes.

Finished Measurement

Sole measures 3 (3¾, 4½) inches

Materials

- Light weight Bernat Softee Baby yarn (5 oz/455 yds per skein): 1 skein prettiest pink #30205
- Size 6 (4.25mm) knitting needles or size needed to obtain gauge
- Tapestry needle
- 2 (½-inch diameter) buttons

Gauge

24 sts and 44 rows = 4 inches/10cm in garter st
To save time, take time to check gauge.

Special Abbreviation

Inc (Increase):
Inc 1 st by knitting in front and back of next st.

Instructions

Left Bootie

Cast on 27 (31, 33) sts.

Row 1 (WS): Knit across.

Row 2 (RS): [K1, inc, k10 (12, 13) sts, inc] twice; k1. (31, 35, 37 sts)

Rows 3, 5, and 7: Knit across.

Row 4: [K1, inc, k12 (14, 15) sts, inc] twice, k1. (35, 39, 41 sts)

Row 6: [K1, inc, k14 (16, 17) sts, inc] twice, k1. (39, 43, 45 sts)

Row 8: K18 (20, 21) sts, inc, k1, inc, k18 (20, 21) sts. (41, 45, 47 sts)

Work 11 rows even in Garter st.

Shape Instep

K23 (25, 26) sts, k2tog, turn, leaving rem sts unworked.

Next row: Sl 1, k5, k2tog, turn, leaving rem sts unworked.

Rep last row until there are 11 (12, 13) sts on each side, then knit to end of row. (29, 31, 33 sts)

Next row: K16 (17, 18) sts, turn.

Strap Loop

Row 1: K3, turn.

Rep Row 1 until strap measures approx 2 inches. Bind off.

Join yarn to sts on side of bootie.

Bind off.

Rep on other side of bootie.

Assembly

Sew sole and heel seam.

Ankle Strap

With RS facing, beg 4 sts to the right of heel seam, pick up and knit 4 sts, pick up and knit 1 st in heel seam, pick up and knit 1 st in each of next 4 sts to left of heel seam. (9 sts)

Next row: Cast on 4 sts, knit across, turn and cast on 20 sts. (33 sts)

Knit 5 rows.

Bind off loosely.

Right Bootie

Work as for left bootie to ankle strap.

Ankle Strap

With RS facing, beg 4 sts to right side of heel seam, pick up and knit 4 sts, pick up and knit 1 st in heel seam, pick up and knit 1 st in each of next 4 sts to left of heel seam. (9 sts)

Next row: Cast on 20 sts, knit across, turn and cast on 4 sts. (33 sts)

Knit 5 rows.

Bind off loosely.

Finishing

Overlap ends of strap and attach button, sewing through all thicknesses. Fold strap loop in half over ankle strap towards the WS and sew in place.

Fur-Trimmed Booties

INTERMEDIATE

Sizes

3–6 (6–9, 9–12) months
Instructions are given for smallest size, with larger sizes in parentheses. When only 1 number is given, it applies to all sizes.

Finished Measurement

Sole measures 3 (3¾, 4½) inches

Materials

- Light weight Patons Astra yarn (1.75 oz/133 yds per skein): 1 skein lip pink #02895 (A) **3 LIGHT**
- Bulky weight Patons Twister yarn (1.75 oz/47yds per skein): 1 skein fruit loops #05711 (B) **6 SUPER BULKY**
- Size 4 (3.5mm) knitting needles or size needed to obtain gauge
- Tapestry needle
- 1 yd (¼-wide) yellow ribbon
- Sewing needle and matching thread

Gauge

22 sts and 28 rows = 4 inches/10cm in St st
To save time, take time to check gauge.

Instructions

Cuff

With B, cast on 22 (22, 24) sts

Work in K1, P1 Rib for approx ½ inch, ending with a WS row.

Next row (RS): Change to A, knit, inc 11 sts evenly spaced across row. (33, 33, 35 sts)

Continue in K1, P1 Rib until cuff measures approx 1 inch, ending with a WS row.

Next row (RS): Knit across.

Next row: Purl across.

Shape Instep

Next row (RS): Knit across.

Next row: P22 (22, 23), turn, leaving rem sts unworked.

Next row: K11, turn, leaving rem sts unworked.

Working on these 11 sts only, continue in St st for 9 (11, 13) rows.

Next row (RS): K1, ssk, knit to last 3 sts, k2tog, k1. (9 sts)

Next row: Purl across.

[Rep last 2 rows] once. (7 sts)

Cut yarn.

With WS facing, join yarn to 11 (11, 12) sts on LH needle and purl across.

Next row (RS): K11 (11, 12), pick up and knit 10 (12, 13) sts evenly spaced across right side of instep, knit across next 7 sts, pick up and knit 10 (12, 13) sts evenly spaced across left side of instep, knit across rem 11 (11, 12) sts. (49, 53, 57 sts)

Work even in St st for 5 (7, 7) rows.

Shape Foot

Row 1: K1, skp, k17 (19, 21), skp, k5, k2tog, k17 (19, 21), k2tog, k1. (45, 49, 53 sts)

Rows 2, 4 and 6: Knit across.

Row 3: K1, skp, k16 (18, 20), skp, k3 k2tog, k16 (18, 20), k2tog, k1. (41, 45, 49 sts)

Row 5: K1, skp, k15 (17, 19), skp, k1, k2tog, k15 (17, 19), k2tog, k1. (37, 41, 45 sts)

Row 7: K1, skp, k14 (16, 18), sk2p, k14 (16, 18), k2tog, k1. (33, 37, 41 sts)

Bind off.

Finishing

Sew foot and back seam. Cut ribbon into 2, ½ yard lengths. Tie each length in a bow and sew to front of bootie.

Nautical Stripe Booties

INTERMEDIATE

Sizes

3–6 (6–9, 9-12) months
Instructions are given for smallest size, with larger sizes in parentheses. When only 1 number is given, it applies to all sizes.

Finished Measurement

Sole measures 3 (3¾, 4½) inches

Materials

- Medium weight TLC Cotton Plus yarn (3.5 oz/140 yds per skein): 1 skein each navy #3859 (A), med blue #3811 (B) and white #3001 (C)
- Size 5 (3.75mm) knitting needles
- Size 6 (4.25mm) knitting needles or size needed to obtain gauge
- Tapestry needle

4 MEDIUM

Gauge

22 sts and 30 rows = 4 inches/10cm in St st with larger needles
To save time, take time to check gauge.

Special Abbreviation

Inc (Increase):
Inc 1 st by knitting in front and back of next st.

Pattern Stitches

Stripe Pattern
Worked in St st
2 rows C
2 rows B
2 rows A

K 1, P 1 Rib
(odd number of sts)
Row 1: K1, *p1, k1; rep from * across.
Row 2: P1, *k1, p1; rep from * across.

Instructions

Sole

With A and larger needles, cast on 25 (29, 35) sts.
Row 1 (RS): [K1, inc, k9 (11, 14) sts, inc] twice, k1. (29, 33, 39 sts)
Rows 2, 4, 6, and 8: Knit across.
Row 3: [K1, inc, k11 (13, 16) sts, inc] twice, k1. (33, 37, 43 sts)
Row 5: [K1, inc, k13 (15, 18) sts, inc] twice, k1. (37, 41, 47 sts)
Row 7: K17 (19, 22) sts, inc, k1, inc, k17 (19, 22). (39, 43, 49 sts)
Join C and work 6 rows even in Stripe pat.

Shape Instep

Set up row: With A, k22 (24, 28) sts, k2tog-tbl, turn, leaving rem sts unworked.
Row 1 (WS): Sl 1, p5 (5, 7) sts, p2tog, turn, leaving rem sts unworked.
Row 2 (RS): Sl 1, k5 (5, 7) sts, k2tog-tbl, turn, leaving rem sts unworked.
[Rep rows 1 and 2] until 9 (11, 10) sts rem on each side. (25, 29, 29 sts)

Next row (RS): Turn, knit across instep and next 9 (11, 10) sts.

Next row: Purl across.

Eyelet row: With C, k2, [k2tog, yo] to last st, k1.

Next row: Purl across.

Cuff

Change to B and smaller needles.

Work in K1, P1 Rib for approx 1½ inches, ending with a WS row.

Next row (RS): Purl across for turning ridge.

Continue in K1, P1 Rib until cuff measures approx 2½ inches from beg, ending with a WS row.

Bind off.

Finishing

Sew foot and back seam, sewing cuff seam from RS for folded area.

Ties

Using 1 strand each of A, B, and C, braid 18 (18, 19) inch length for tie. Tie overhand knot at each end and trim. Beginning and ending at center front, weave tie through eyelet row and tie in bow.

Repeat for other bootie.

Cabled Booties

INTERMEDIATE

Sizes

3–6 (6–9, 9–12) months
Instructions are given for smallest size, with larger sizes in parentheses. When only 1 number is given, it applies to all sizes.

Finished Measurement

Sole measures 3 (3¾, 4½) inches

Materials

- Light weight Bernat Softee Baby yarn (5 oz/455 yds per skein): 1 skein baby denim #30184
- Size 5 (3.25mm) knitting needles
- Size 6 (4.25mm) knitting needles or size needed to obtain gauge
- Cable needle (cn)
- 2 stitch markers
- Tapestry needle

Gauge

22 sts and 30 rows = 4 inches/10cm in St st with larger needles
To save time, take time to check gauge.

Special Abbreviation

M1 (Make 1):

Insert LH needle under horizontal thread between st just worked and next st, knit through the back loop.

Pattern Stitches

Baby Cable Rib

(multiple of 4 sts + 2)

Row 1 (WS): K2, *p2, k2; rep from * across.

Row 2 (RS): P2, *k2, p2; rep from * across.

Row 3: Rep Row 1.

Row 4: P2, *k2tog and leave sts on needle, insert right needle between the 2 sts knit tog into first st and knit first st again, slipping both sts from needle tog, p2; rep from * across row.

Simple Cable Pattern

(multiple of 8 sts)

Row 1 (WS): K2, p4, k2.

Row 2 (RS): P2, k4, p2.

Row 3: K2, p4, k2.

Row 4: P2, sl next 2 sts to cn and hold in back, k2, then k2 from cn, p2.

Rep Rows 1–4 for pat.

Instructions

Cuff

With smaller needles, cast on 38 (38, 42) sts.

Work [Rows 1–4 of Baby Cable rib] 3 times.

Work Row 1 of Baby Cable rib.

Change to larger needles.

Next row (RS): K4 (4, 2) sts, k2tog, [k2 sts, k2tog] 7 (7, 9) times, k4 (4, 2) sts. (30, 30, 32 sts)

Set Up Cable Pat

Next row (WS): P11 (11, 12), place marker, work Row 1 of Simple Cable pat over next 8 sts, place marker, purl 11 (11, 12) sts.

Note: Work Simple Cable pat between markers throughout.

Shape Instep

Next row (RS): Work in Simple Cable pat across.

Next row: Work in pat across 21 (21, 22) sts, turn, leaving rem sts unworked.

Next row: Work in pat across 12 sts, turn, leaving rem sts unworked.

Working on these 12 sts only, continue in pat for 9 (11, 13) rows.

Next row (RS): K1, ssk, knit to last 3 sts, k2tog, k1. (10 sts)

Next row: Work in pat across.

Note: Remove markers while working next row.

Next row (RS): P1, p2tog, work to last 3 sts, p2 tog, p1. (8 sts)

Cut yarn.

With WS facing, join yarn to 9 (9, 10) sts on LH needle and purl across.

Next row (RS): K9 (9, 10), pick up and knit 10 (12, 13) sts evenly spaced across right side of instep, place marker, continue in cable pat across next 8 sts, place marker, pick up and knit 10 (12, 13) sts evenly spaced across left side of instep, knit across rem 9 (9, 10) sts. (46, 50, 54 sts)

Continue to work in pats as established for 5 (7, 7) rows.

Next row (RS): Bind off 19 (21, 23) sts, remove marker, continue in Simple Cable pat across center 8 sts, remove marker, bind off rem 19 (21, 23) sts.

Shape Sole

Join yarn to rem 8 sts.

Continue in Simple Cable pat and *at the same time* inc (by M1) each end [every 3rd (4th, 3rd) row] 4 (4, 6) times, working inc sts in rev St st (purl on RS, knit on WS). (16, 16, 20 sts)

Dec (by k2 tog) each end [every 3rd (4th, 3rd) row] 4 (4, 6) times. (8 sts)

Bind off.

Finishing

Sew heel seam. Sew sides of bootie and sole tog.

EASY

Sizes

3–6 (6–9) months
Instructions are given for smallest size, with larger sizes in parentheses. When only 1 number is given, it applies to both sizes.

Finished Measurement

Sole measures 3¾ (4¼) inches

Materials

- Light weight Red Heart Soft Baby yarn (7 oz/594 yds per skein): 1 skein each sky blue #7822 (A) and lime #7624 (B)
- Size 6 (4.25mm) knitting needles or size needed to obtain gauge
- Tapestry needle
- 1 yd (⅜-inch wide) ribbon

Gauge

24 sts and 32 rows = 4 inches/10cm in St st
To save time, take time to check gauge.

Special Abbreviation

Inc (Increase):
Inc 1 by working in the front and back of next st.

Pattern Stitches

Stripe Pattern
* 2 rows A
2 rows B
Rep from * for pat.

K1, P1 Rib
(even number of sts)
Row 1 (RS): *K1, p1; rep from * across.
Rep Row 1 for pat.

Instructions

Sole

With A, cast on 15 (18) sts.

Working Stripe pat in St st, inc 1 st each end [every row] 3 times, then [every other row] once. (23, 26 sts)

Continuing in Stripe pat work 3 (5) rows even.

Dec row (RS): K2tog, knit to last 2 sts, k2tog. (21, 24 sts)

Rep Dec row [every other row] once, then [every row] twice. (15, 18 sts)

Bind off.

Upper Section

Hold with RS facing, with A, pick up and knit 3 (5) sts from 1 short end of sole (for toe).

Toe

Row 1 and all odd-numbered rows: Purl across.

Row 2: K1 st, [inc] 2 (3) times, k0 (1) sts. (5, 8 sts)

Row 4: K1 (2) sts, [inc] 3 (4) times, k1 (2) sts. (8, 12 sts)

Row 6: K2 (4) sts, [inc] 5 (5) times, k1 (3) sts. (13, 17 sts)

Row 8: K4 (6) sts, [inc] 6 (6) times, k3 (5) sts. (19, 23 sts)

Row 9: Purl across.

Work 12 rows even in St st.

Next row (RS): K8 (10) sts, bind off center 3 sts, work rem sts.

First Side

Working on last 8 (10) sts, work 1 row even.

Dec row (RS): K1, ssk, k5 (7). (7, 9 sts)

Rep Dec row [every other row] twice. (5, 7 sts)

Work 9 (10) rows even.

Bind off.

2nd Side

Hold with WS facing, join A to rem 8 (10) sts, and work 1 row even.

Dec row (RS): Knit to last 3 sts, k2tog, k1. (7, 9 sts)

Rep Dec row [every other row] twice. (5, 7 sts)

Work 9 (10) rows even.

Bind off.

Edging

Hold with RS facing, with B pick up and knit 28 (30) sts around ankle edge. Work in K1, P1 Rib for approx ½ inch, ending with a WS row. Bind off loosely in ribbing.

Finishing

Sew heel seam. Sew sides of bootie and sole tog.

With 1 strand each of A and B, make two small 1-inch pompoms for each bootie. Cut ribbon in two 18-inch lengths. Tie each length in bow. Referring to photo for placement, sew bow to bootie and attach pompoms.

Play-Date Booties

EASY

Sizes

Newborn (3–6, 6–9) months
Instructions are given for smallest size, with larger sizes in parentheses. When only 1 number is given, it applies to all sizes.

Finished Measurement

Sole measures 2¾ (3, 3½) inches

Materials

- Medium weight Red Heart Baby Econo yarn (6 oz/480 yds per skein): 1 skein each baby green #1682 (A) and rainbow sherbet #1982 (B)

  4 MEDIUM
- Size 6 (4.25mm) knitting needles or size needed to obtain gauge
- Tapestry needle
- 2 (½-inch wide) buttons

Gauge

20 sts and 28 rows = 4 inches/10cm in St st
To save time, take time to check gauge.

Special Abbreviation

Inc (Increase):
Inc 1 by knitting in front and back of next st.

Instructions

Left Bootie

With A, cast on 23 (27, 29) sts.

Row 1 (WS): Knit across.

Row 2 (RS): [K1, inc, k8 (10, 11) sts, inc] twice, k1. (27, 31, 33 sts)

Row 3: Knit across.

Row 4: [K1, inc, k10 (12, 13) sts, inc 1] twice, k1. (31, 35, 37 sts)

Row 5: Knit across.

For Newborn Size Only:

Row 6: [K1, inc, k12, inc] twice, k1. (35 sts)

For 3–6 Months and 6–9 Months Sizes Only:

Row 6: K16 (17) sts, inc, k1, inc, K 16 (17) sts. (37, 39 sts)

For All Sizes:

Row 7 (WS): With B, purl across.

Work 10 rows in St st.

Shape Instep

Set- Up row (RS): K20 (21, 22) sts, k2tog, turn, leaving rem sts unworked.

Row 1: Sl 1, p5 sts, p2tog, turn, leaving rem sts unworked.

Row 2: Sl 1, k5 sts, k2tog, turn, leaving rem sts unworked.

[Rep Row 1 and 2] until 9 (10, 11) sts rem on each side. (25, 27, 29 sts)

Bind off instep and side sts. Cut yarn.

Join yarn and bind off rem side sts.

Assembly

Sew sole and heel seam.

Ankle Strap

With RS facing, beg 4 sts to right of heel seam, pick up and knit 4 sts, pick up and knit 1 st in heel seam, pick up and knit 4 sts to left of heel seam. (9 sts)

Next row: Cast on 4 sts, and knit across, turn and cast on 20 sts. (33 sts)

Knit 2 rows, ending at end of short side of strap.

Next row: Work to last 4 sts, k2tog, yo, k2 (for buttonhole).

Knit 2 rows.

Bind off loosely.

Right Bootie

Work as for left bootie to Ankle Strap

Ankle Strap

With RS facing, beg 4 sts to right of heel seam, pick up and knit 4 sts, pick up and knit 1 st in heel seam, pick up and knit 4 sts to left of heel seam. (9 sts)

Next row: Cast on 20 sts, knit across, turn and cast on 4 sts. (33 sts)

Knit 2 rows, ending at end of long side of strap. K2, yo, k2tog (buttonhole), knit across.

Knit 2 rows.

Bind off loosely.

Finishing

Sew buttons to end of short side of straps.

Ballet Slippers

EASY

Sizes

3–6 (6–12) months
Instructions are given for smallest size, with larger size in parentheses. When only 1 number is given, it applies to both sizes.

Finished Measurements

Sole measures 3¾ (4¼) inches

Materials

- Light weight Lion Brand yarn (5 oz/459 yd per skein): 1 skein bubble gum #103
- Size 3 (3.25mm) knitting needles
- Size 4 (3.5mm) knitting needles
- Size 5 (3.75mm) knitting needles or size needed to obtain gauge
- Tapestry needle
- 1 yard ribbon

Gauge

24 sts and 32 rows = 4 inches/10cm in St st with size 5 needles
To save time, take time to check gauge.

Special Abbreviation

Inc (Increase):

Inc 1 st by knitting in front and back of next st.

Instructions

Sole

With size 5 needles, cast on 15 (18) sts.

Work in St st, inc 1 st each end [every row] 3 times, then [every other row] once. (23, 26 sts)

Work 3 (5) rows even.

Dec row (RS): K2tog, work in pat to last 2 sts, k2tog. (21, 24 sts)

Continuing in St st work Dec row [every other row] once, then [every row] twice. (15, 18 sts)
Bind off.

Top of Foot

With size 5 needles, and RS facing, pick up and knit 3 (5) sts across 1 short end of sole for toe.

Row 1 and all odd-numbered rows (WS): Purl.

Row 2 (RS): K1 st, [inc] 2 (3) times, k0 (1) sts. (5, 8 sts)

Row 4: K1 (2) sts, [inc] 3 (4) times, k1 (2) sts. (8, 12 sts)

Row 6: K2 (4) sts, [inc] 5 (5) times, k1 (3) sts. (13, 17 sts)

Row 8: K4 (6) sts, [inc] 6 (6) times, k3 (5) sts. (19, 23 sts)

Row 9: Purl.

Row 10: Knit.

Row 11: Purl.

[Rep Rows 10 and 11] 6 times.

Next row (RS): K8 (10) sts, bind off center 3 sts, work across rem sts.

Working on last 8 (10) sts only, purl 1 row even.

Dec row (RS): K1, ssk, k5 (7). (7, 9 sts)

Rep Dec row [every other row] twice. (5, 7 sts)

Work 9 (11) rows even. Bind off.

With WS facing, join yarn to rem 8 (10) sts, and purl 1 row even.

Dec row (RS): Knit to last 3 sts, k2tog, k1. (7, 9 sts)

Rep Dec row [every other row] twice. (5, 7 sts)

Work 9 (13) rows even.

Bind off.

Picot Cuff

With size 4 needles and RS facing, pick up and knit 30 sts around ankle edge. Work 3 rows even in St st.

Ribbon Eyelet row: K5, [k2tog, yo, k4] 3 times, k2tog, yo, k5.

Continue even in St st until cuff measures approx 1 inch.

Picot Turning Ridge: K1, *yo, k2tog; rep from * across, ending k1.

Change to size 3 needles and continue even in St st for approx 1 inch, ending with a WS row. Bind off loosely.

Finishing

Sew heel seam. Sew sides of bootie and sole tog, easing in any fullness at toe.

Fold cuff hem inside at picot turning ridge, pin and sew in place.

Cut ribbon into 2 18-inch lengths. Weave 1 length through eyelet row of each bootie and tie bow.

Ballet Leggings

BEGINNER

Size

6–12 months

Finished Measurements

Circumference at ankle: 6½ inches
Circumference at knee: 8½ inches
Length: 7½ inches

Materials

- Light weight Lion Brand yarn (5 oz/459 yds per skein): 1 skein each bubble gum #103 (A) and pastel pink #101 (B)
- Size 4 (3.5mm) knitting needles
- Size 5 (3.75mm) knitting needles or size needed to obtain gauge
- Tapestry needle

Gauge

24 sts and 32 rows = 4 inches/10cm in St st with larger needles
To save time, take time to check gauge.

Special Abbreviation

M1 (Make 1):
Insert LH needle under horizontal thread between st just worked and next st, knit through the back loop.

Pattern Stitch

K1, P1 Rib
(odd number of sts)
Row 1 (RS): *K1, p1; rep from * to last st, k1.
Row 2: P1, *k1, p1; rep from * across.

Instructions

With larger needles and B, loosely cast on 39 sts.

Change to A, and work in K1, P1 Rib for approx ½ inch, ending with a WS row.

Next row (RS): Work in St st, inc (by M1) each end [every fourth row] once, [every sixth row] twice, [every eighth row] twice, then [every tenth row] once. (51 sts)

Work even until piece measures approx 7½ inches from beg, ending with a WS row.

Change to smaller needles.

Work in K1, P1 Rib for approx ½ inch, ending with a WS row.

Change to B and bind off loosely in rib.

Finishing

Sew leg seam.

Abbreviations & Symbols

approx	approximately
beg	begin/beginning
CC	contrasting color
ch	chain stitch
cm	centimeter(s)
cn	cable needle
dec	decrease/decreases/decreasing
dpn(s)	double-pointed needle(s)
g	gram
inc	increase/increases/increasing
k	knit
k2tog	knit 2 stitches together
LH	left hand
lp(s)	loop(s)
m	meter(s)
M1	make one stitch
MC	main color
mm	millimeter(s)
oz	ounce(s)
p	purl
pat(s)	pattern(s)
p2tog	purl 2 stitches together
psso	pass slipped stitch over
p2sso	pass 2 slipped stitches over
rem	remain/remaining
rep	repeat(s)
rev St st	reverse stockinette stitch
RH	right hand

rnd(s)	rounds
RS	right side
skp	slip, knit, pass stitch over—one stitch decreased
sk2p	slip 1, knit 2 together, pass slip stitch over the knit 2 together; 2 stitches have been decreased
sl	slip
sl 1k	slip 1 knitwise
sl 1p	slip 1 purlwise
sl st	slip stitch(es)
ssk	slip, slip, knit these 2 stitches together—a decrease
st(s)	stitch(es)
St st	stockinette stitch/stocking stitch
tbl	through back loop(s)
tog	together
WS	wrong side
wyib	with yarn in back
wyif	with yarn in front
yd(s)	yard(s)
yfwd	yarn forward
yo	yarn over

[ ] work instructions within brackets as many times as directed

( ) work instructions within parentheses in the place directed

** repeat instructions following the asterisks as directed

* repeat instructions following the single asterisk as directed

" inch(es)

How to Check Gauge

A correct stitch gauge is very important. Please take the time to work a stitch-gauge swatch about 4 x 4 inches. Measure the swatch. If the number of stitches and rows are fewer than indicated under "Gauge" in the pattern, your needles are too large. Try another swatch with smaller-size needles. If the number of stitches and rows are more than indicated under "Gauge" in the pattern, your needles are too small. Try another swatch with larger-size needles.

Twisted Cord

Cut a 3-yard length of each yarn indicated. Tie 1 end to a door handle or hook. Twist the strands counterclockwise until yarn kinks up on itself when it relaxes. Hold yarn at middle of twisted strand, remove end from handle and allow yarn to twist back on itself.

Pompoms

Cut two cardboard circles in size specified in pattern. Cut a hole in the center of each circle, about ½ inch in diameter. Thread a tapestry needle with a length of yarn doubled. Holding both circles together, insert needle through center hole, over the outside edge, through center again (Fig. 1) until entire circle is covered and center hole is filled (thread more length of yarn as needed).

Using two 12-inch strands of yarn, slip yarn between circles and overlap yarn ends two or three times (Fig. 3) to prevent knot from slipping, pull tightly and tie into a firm knot. Remove cardboard and fluff out pompom by rolling it between your hands. Trim even with scissors and leave the tying ends for attaching pompom to project.

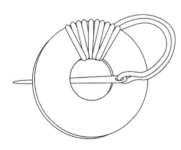

Fig. 1

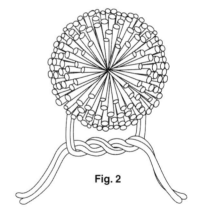

Fig. 2

With sharp scissors, cut yarn between the two circles all around the circumference (Fig. 2).

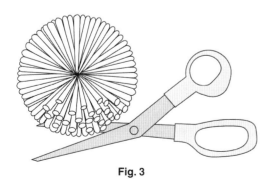

Fig. 3

Metric Charts

INCHES INTO MILLIMETERS & CENTIMETERS (Rounded off slightly)

inches	mm	cm	inches	cm	inches	cm	inches	cm
1/8	3	0.3	5	12.5	21	53.5	38	96.5
1/4	6	0.6	5 1/2	14	22	56	39	99
3/8	10	1	6	15	23	58.5	40	101.5
1/2	13	1.3	7	18	24	61	41	104
5/8	15	1.5	8	20.5	25	63.5	42	106.5
3/4	20	2	9	23	26	66	43	109
7/8	22	2.2	10	25.5	27	68.5	44	112
1	25	2.5	11	28	28	71	45	114.5
1 1/4	32	3.2	12	30.5	29	73.5	46	117
1 1/2	38	3.8	13	33	30	76	47	119.5
1 3/4	45	4.5	14	35.5	31	79	48	122
2	50	5	15	38	32	81.5	49	124.5
2 1/2	65	6.5	16	40.5	33	84	50	127
3	75	7.5	17	43	34	86.5		
3 1/2	90	9	18	46	35	89		
4	100	10	19	48.5	36	91.5		
4 1/2	115	11.5	20	51	37	94		

KNITTING NEEDLE CONVERSION CHART

U.S.	1	2	3	4	5	6	7	8	9	10	10 1/2	11	13	15	17	19	35	50
Continental-mm	2.25	2.75	3.25	3.5	3.75	4	4.5	5	5.5	6	6.5	8	9	10	12.75	15	19	25

Standard Yarn Weight System

Categories of yarn, gauge ranges, and recommended needle sizes

Yarn Weight Symbol & Category Names	1 SUPER FINE	2 FINE	3 LIGHT	4 MEDIUM	5 BULKY	6 SUPER BULKY
Type of Yarns in Category	Sock, Fingering, Baby	Sport, Baby	DK, Light Worsted	Worsted, Afghan, Aran	Chunky, Craft, Rug	Bulky, Roving
Knit Gauge Range* in Stockinette Stitch to 4 inches	27–32 sts	23–26 sts	21–24 sts	16–20 sts	12–15 sts	6–11 sts
Recommended Needle in Metric Size Range	2.25–3.25mm	3.25–3.75mm	3.75–4.5mm	4.5–5.5mm	5.5–8mm	8mm and larger
Recommended Needle U.S. Size Range	1 to 3	3 to 5	5 to 7	7 to 9	9 to 11	11 and larger

* GUIDELINES ONLY: The above reflect the most commonly used gauges and needle sizes for specific yarn categories.

Skill Levels

BEGINNER
Beginner projects for first-time knitters using basic stitches. Minimal shaping.

EASY
Easy projects using basic stitches, repetitive stitch patterns, simple color changes and simple shaping and finishing.

INTERMEDIATE
Intermediate projects with a variety of stitches, mid-level shaping and finishing.

EXPERIENCED
Experienced projects using advanced techniques and stitches, detailed shaping and refined finishing.

DRG Publishing
306 East Parr Road
Berne, IN 46711
©2006 American School of Needlework

TOLL-FREE ORDER LINE or to request a free catalog (800) 582-6643
Customer Service (800) 282-6643, **Fax** (800) 882-6643

Visit AnniesAttic.com.

ISBN: 978-1-59012-181-8   All rights reserved.   Printed in USA   4 5 6 7 8 9